MARVELUS

Founded during the COVID-19 pandemic, the Oklahoma Prison Writers and Artists Foundation is a 501(c)3 organization that supports and promotes writers and artists working in the Oklahoma prison system. OPWAF recognizes the liberatory, healing and humanizing power of the creative process; our mission is to serve as a conduit between incarcerated creators and wider public audiences. We are proud to present Dilemma's collection *MarvelUs,* the first in *Emerging Voices,* a series of volumes by writers incarcerated in Oklahoma. Our thanks to Jeanetta Calhoun Mish of Mongrel Empire Press for permission to republish "Figures," which previously appeared in *Emergence*, a collection by the JHCC Writers Guild.

MARVELUS

POEMS

DILEMMA

...

OPWAF EDITIONS

INDEMIONA
IN'DAYVIONIA
LYRIC
DEODRIAN
LAMAREA
KING
ZA'VIONA
TI'KURIOUS

ABOUT THE AUTHOR

I am Dilemma yet I'm not the problem society is

I'm a father of six beautiful children who are the light of my life

I am a Christian but more importantly

I am a misunderstood African-American inmate in a system meant to keep me down...

But it can't. I'm too MarvelUs!

ACKNOWLEDGMENTS

I would like to thank Catherine Mintler, Tim Bradford, Ben and Ashlyn Winters, OK Message Project Executive Director Cheri Fuller, Michele Eodice, Ms. Wonderful, Mr. Washington, anonymous kquote, Luke Sinclair, Keith Bonner, Rico Cruz, my brothers Shannon Hunt, Frederick "P" Watson, Chris "X" Benson, Zachary Buchanan, Morye Chandler, Kristi and Jemal Hatcher, my sister Danielle Mungo, and my mother Lynnette Mungo for doing the best she could. Thanks to my mentor Nick LoLordo for his help at every step of the process. Thanks to the Writers Guild and the Oklahoma Prison Writers and Artists Foundation.

CONTENTS

MARVELUS

MARVELUS

When I RED another WHITE cop BLUE another black man away there went another **Captain America**,

That's because being black will get you capped in America,

But then they ask for peaceful protest...they want us to sit back and settle,

The police kin to **Magneto**...because they don't mind using that metal,

We have a **Vision** and the movement we on is **Colossus** though nothing less than incredible,

So l hope they keep they nose (**Thanos**) clean...because us snapping is inevitable,

But they think it's **The Thing** to do...kill blacks...man you all need some help,

I just don't understand how someone so foul can (**Falcon**) live with themselves,

They may have had it rough but ours is no movie either if so it'd be a sick thriller,

We get no breaks, the Judge and the DA involved in our demise just to get some **Quick Silver**,

They gave us no choice but to react like this through this **Storm** we hate,

They played **Gambit**...so they knew the cards we were dealt were going to blow up in our face,

They say something's wrong with us and we low key (**Loki**) need counseling but I rather go to God and pray,

Because them telling me it's my fault will have me looking at the **Dr. Strange**,

I just keep the facts real though and I don't lack skill so,

I rather tell the truth so you'll see why she drunk off **Incredible Hulk** not only because she feel low...

It's also now because she's become a **Black Widow**.

By: Dilemma
A.k.a. StrokeGameVicious

REACHING

I wanna start off by saying I may lose some people by my analogies,
metaphors and similes,
Maybe that's why a lot of people are not into to me but that's what God put
into me,
A lot of things on my mind Lord...the fruit of my labor shows everything's
Kosher,
But I don't want to be dead weight, because there's way too many vultures,
I mean I wanna carry my own weight...but I'm trying to do it sober,
See we all got the same drive...but some of us still asking for a chauffeur,
Why? When some of us the next up plus God done blessed us,
It's Easy math...The Problem is we can't see...basically Da vision messed up,
That's messed up...because He gave us the necessary tools to light others,
And to help us get to higher heights...He put us around the Wright
Brothers,
And sisters...Also God is Notorious for the analogical things He'd say,
I say Notorious because it's ironic how it's so BIG to believe in FAITH,
We were already separated but now we got the Bible to involve our minds,
But when we gotta stand up here with His writing it's like a hyphen...
Because that's where we'll draw the line,
Think computers...God monitors us that's why His children screen us
today,
Because you gang bang and thinking you holding on to the right click...til it
get you dragged away,
He wants us in Order 'cause we're all on the menu to serve Him better,
Take the word menu for instance...That's only because he wants me n u
together,
So don't act like we not the problem,
We His children,
So it's apparent that God's the Father,

We got a choice to be in a relationship with Him no need to ask,

He's a gentleman who shows Grace we're not puppets...so there's No strings attached,

There will be miles of innovations,

Trials and tribulations,

That causes an invocation,

To God for ventilation,

Basically there will be new things you encounter and things that you went through,

That has you praying to God because He's the person to vent to,

Because he never said that it'd be easy...and yes He can make Mountains move,

But you want the truth? You will suffer as he suffered too...

It's like Elementary School students...you got your work cut out for you,

Now before you clap I don't want to take full credit as the Author,

Because while you're thanking me I'm thanking my Father

By: Dilemma

A.k.a. StrokeGameVicious

FIGURES...

I'm trying to be a better father figure,

Since I figured my father didn't want to bother with us,

Was tired of living back and forth without a pot to piss in,

I got so used to moving I can't say it's not addictive,

It never was a thought that I would mimic,

The same footsteps once I looked back...shoot my father did it,

Still have no idea who he is though my pops was missin',

I made every effort to not be in my pops' position,

I felt just like my father...figures,

I didn't see this coming...feel like l lost the vision,

But am I the victim?

Naw...and time is ticking,

And change was supposed to start with me but I reside in prison,

But now my mind has shifted,

I'm thinking outside of the box this time instead of climbing in it,

I'll defy the limit and expectations the system said that I couldn't finish,

I'm not a number and I'm not gone succumb to the opposition,

Of me being a person because of a cop's intentions,

I'm not gone listen nor make any propositions with no politicians,

So they can take their loud malicious gossip with 'em,

I've suffered enough consequences,

But how do we get even when the odds against us,

Common sense would say stop pretending,

Like everything is ok when this box we live in,

Is so infected by greed we need amoxicillin,

It's funny how violence is not offensive,

It's become the norm like washing dishes or prisons with locks & fences,

Hands up don't shoot that's what was brought to millions,

Yet we still can't stop the killin',

Whether it's now or back then there's not a difference,
From being shot by a cop or lynching,
This the generation my kids growing up in and it's not appealin',
No need to block the feelin',
Because they so used to it that it doesn't shock the children,
Crazy isn't it?
Figures...

By: Dilemma
A.k.a. StrokeGameVicious

MORE THAN A NUMBER

I am more than a number...
You say be grateful as if we are all hateful but I resent the latter,
As a matter of fact we can't have an opinion on any matter because we don't matter,
People want us to be quiet...as if we lost our right to speak,
Respond? That type of speech will ignite a fight if we don't be silent and accept defeat,
Defeat? That notion assumes that we loss just because of the temporary place we reside,
One bad decision will never define our lives,
You say you proud,
Yet you steady burying me underground,
You gone take me to an early grave from the way that you sound,
Because you treat me like a coffin...how you lift me up just to let me down,
Rehabilitation is the illustration you want to provide,
But you rather kill us because your love of money is worth more than us being alive,
The system are the biggest criminals...all you do is integrate to manipulate,
Keeping us in prison knowing the gravity of our mistakes will help take up space,
If these 4 walls could talk....
But this book is about me
I rather spend less time talking about you
That's all!

By: Dilemma
A.k.a. StrokeGameVicious

LAYERS

You are beautiful...perfection,

But we are in this mask era where mascara can mask error,

But it is only an error when it needs correction,

And no makeup can make up for the make-up of your DNA,

You rather wear weave than braids cause we enslaved,

We are suffering and I gotta put to sleep the lies and look the youth in eyes

And euthanize the you an Is that thinks it's ok for you to hide the truth inside,

Let's get down to business...

I'm severing ties from several lives

Because I have to ignore the current and not go with the current who follow the tide,

We drowning...

And the life raft might have a hole in it,

All because society "ACT" like they care...their stage presence play a role in it,

From the commercials that tell you what beauty looks like,

To the most expensive clothing being the only thing that makes you look nice,

How shallow!

I'm pissed...you know...urinate,

On a scale from 1 to hate you're an eight,

And that hate is passed down because you're innate,

But we allow influence to ensue us and we turn around to meet it,

And what you found indecent is now worth keeping since you've denounced those demons,

It's like division...

We are the divisors...the dividends are worldly possessions

And the quotients are the people who tell you what's hot or not,

Basically they want to put worldly possessions in a box and see how they can

fit you in it so they can come out on top,

Be who you are...and don't initiate hate

People may try and branch out but remember even trees provide shade,

Stay cool...

You can only be you

So don't lose yourself trying to prove yourself!

By: Dilemma
A.k.a. StrokeGameVicious

YOU CAN ALWAYS REPLACE A WINDOW

Look at me!
Am I so irrelevant that my melanin's the only place to put metal in from the
metal end that's meddling...?
What have I done so bad that you have the right to decide if I live or die?
These are your words that I'll dissect in verse,
Protect and serve...
Correct those verbs they don't intersect or merge
You reject the sure without connecting first which affects the next to expect
the worse,
We put up walls because we trying to keep our pain on a downward incline,
While you tried to have the blacks molded the way you wanted but it killed
us on the inside,
So you shattering dreams had us shattering things...But!
YOU CAN ALWAYS REPLACE A WINDOW...

You set that example...
To judge because of skin pigment now what lies inward is the N-word,
And you work hard to show it through your actions and we pay for it daily
in turn though you're an intern
You see what's going on in the world and witness all the hatred but don't say
shit,
Just because you're married to your job don't mean you can't learn from
previous engagements,
I'm so sick of people saying be peaceful...
The foundation you want us to stand on is shaky and we just now breaking
ground,
So why should we be worried about a building?
When you continuously tearing us down, But!
YOU CAN ALWAYS REPLACE A WINDOW...

And since you're see through I see threw the evil that leads you,
Your favorite phrase is "I thought they had a"
You thought we had a what?
A pack of skittles? An inhaler? A Taser, brush? A Gun?
What amazed me is that excuse gets you paid leave,
I'm on my couch...
What's equal rights when ten years is worth my life?
If it was me I'd rot in the pen if I mess up and say I thought it was my house,
You only correct your mistakes when it comes to letting someone white out,
We tried to build bridges to get across to you and tell you what's important,
No one listened.
How you expect us to take the stairs to higher heights when you only believe
in one story? But!
YOU CAN ALWAYS REPLACE A WINDOW...

It was dark only because the ceiling was sealing our fate...
But we still on our way even though that steel is still in our way,
Your condolences got me questioning what your motive is because you're
masterminds,
Judgements harsh so we don't get a lower case because you capitalize on
capitol lies,
You tried to keep us in chains...head down with our chin low,
Silent, scared to speak up while locked inside our home,
No doors because you didn't want to provide us a way out so you kept us
enclosed,
And in close the only way is to break free...and since I CAN'T BREATHE...
YOU GONE REPLACE THAT WINDOW...

By: Dilemma
A.k.a. StrokeGameVicious

IN-WARD

Say it!

I know you want to...you got black friends that say it maybe they won't care

So that give you the right to take it and run with it Its your ticket to get in the door it's only fair

That you should be able to use that same term we use as greetings

But where they do that at? At a KKK meeting

You might as well wrap a noose around our neck yourself

We never were friends you really label us as the help

Say it!

It's only ok telling your children under your own roof

Then having them repeating the same word in school

Then when you get the news you act like you're not the reason they're repeating it like it's cool

And your excuse is that's what we say to each other too

But it's different when that same word is coming from you

Well Say It!

But it's ok right?

Is it the wave caps, braided hair backwards hats baggy pants wearing our jeans low?

One hand turning corners at a wide angle using just our palm on the steering wheel slow

Leaning on the driver side door with our head halfway out the window,

Are we proud and cocky or just confident with common sense to know the difference

From you saying it and us calling each other niggas,

So Say IT!

Now clearly we use it as a term of endearment no different

From 2 female friends calling each other bitches

But when you say it how am I supposed to take it?

It wasn't you but someone who looks like you took the negative
connotation and embraced it,
So how we supposed to trust what you said you'd insure when it's impure
And all those lies cover up what lies inward...The N-Word
Just Say it!
I'M SORRY!
Now was that hard?

By: Dilemma
A.k.a. StrokeGameVicious

FRACTURED STATE OF MINE

As I reflect looking at my reflection there's a message we lived,
It's like a C-Section...fuck it let's cut to the chase you gotta open up to get to these kids,
The continuous disrespect is why I dis-connect with society,
Because too many people are getting shot and drug down even when they choose sobriety,
They eyein' me always trying to keep an eye on me,
'Cause I'm in basketball shorts and T instead of a suit and tie on me,
So that give you a reason to lie on me?
I'm not a mattress...so don't get comfortable but it's getting worse now,
Shots coming from everywhere I heard rounds,
And now you ain't gotta go ten yards to be the first down,
Hmph! They say not all cops are racist,
And I say not all blacks are gangstas,
You looking for the bad guy huh...and somehow I fit the description,
They say if the shoe fits wear it...But my toes are bending because you forced me in 'em.
They ask why you write so much stuff about hate Dilemma...Because this is the mindset of where my mind sat,
We build walls to keep those people out but is an inside job...So where do we draw the line at?
It's compact...And now you hate yourself because you're going through hate yourself,
They put that metal to your mouth...then tell you brace yourself,
What type of sh...you know what? If you get offended,
Play the Dentist and get out ya feelings,
'Cause black folks still dyin' and we tired of being quiet,
Sittin' here in silence while you create the violençe,
From start to finish,

The #MeToo marching women,
Children who hearts diminished
From bullying that cause suicidal thought inventions,
Blacks suffering the harshest living,
Getting killed over a gram of weed or parking tickets,
You're ready to open up now huh? Until you're under that blade,
But like Homeroom to first hour...you're subject to change,
That's what they all say...Same ole same ole I know I prolly sound like a broke record,
I thought they'd never give us a chance until we advanced in sports and broke records,
Now you in the front row, blunt smoke, yelling for the black folk,
Baggy pants, tall T, sittin wit ya hat low,
Your best friend's black y'all pointin' tellin' fat jokes,
Don't worry 'cause in the end y'all gone pay...and that's when I'm a act broke,
Think about it....Dilemma!

By: Dilemma
A.k.a. StrokeGameVicious

CONSCIOUSNESS

There's a story behind every line I speak,

Coasting down I-40 with my eye on the 40 from green signs I've seen,

And I'm not drinking either...just being cautious!

Because I'm driving while black and it's a shame,

They call us gang bangers when your wives are to blame,

But just like her we want change...

Or something different,

Because shooting us on camera isn't an act worth living or dying for...

You asked me for non-verbal communication,

Walk backwards, lay on the ground...I CAN'T BREATHE! You didn't notice my body language?

That's not a good excuse.

That's as bad as my dog ate my homework as if that works,

Which it wouldn't because we'd have to make it home from work first,

I had a good friend of mine have us meditate,

At that time, I couldn't concentrate,

But I see death

I hear crying

It's bitterness I taste,

I smell fear

My brother said the touch of a gun is the only time he felt safe,

Now that I think about it...I've never felt truly safe and that's scarier,

If all this hatred came to an immediate stop

The momentum would push us forward shattering all barriers,

No matter how mad we get we need to be better activists,

They planted the seeds that got us killing ourselves.

I know what's Happening, but it's not a movie!

Look at my hands...are they past the legal limit? I meant are they high enough?

Do you have to handle me so rough in these tightened cuffs?
You have to recite the what? Our Miranda Rights?
The man you convicted with no evidence and used his priors to put in jail?
That Miranda? Riigghhtt!
So, it's guilty until proven innocent...
I thought it was already bad enough being under the gun,
But you judged me way before I even stood in front of one,
Bang!
Oh my God!
You fired...but you still got your job!

By: Dilemma
A.k.a. StrokeGameVicious

T. H. U. G.

The Hate U Give makes you not see color...

"Then you don't see me"...that line was great,

They don't see us because they are going for our heart...so lives are at stake,

We're not vampires but still feel like slaves

On a plantation farming...

That's what's been ingrained,

And we walk out our homes peaceful yet feeling like Deebo...

Because we still in chains,

It's like you ready to slap us in cuffs it's sad so

Yeah we rude but subdued though

So, you don't have to keep your hand cocked, assholes,

So why? 'Cause no one ever seems to have an answer,

I'm sick of the slick banter,

So now I'm staying on stage for...

The people who consider us cancer,

It's crazy how we dream about a life with a house and our first fence,

Then we housed with life on our first offense,

'Cause being black was our first offense,

Then like me we grow up as a victim in the system,

The little black kid you need to adopt to fit in,

Teach him about everything but the people born with the same skin,

Saying to us that we can be way better than them,

Oh wow! What a pronoun.

All that baggage just seems like a lot to take in,

Their point of view points at you as the problem...

Better yet the Dilemma that's it,

The center of a sinner and it hurts like a splinter...

So of course that would get under our skin,

You wanted the truth well this me schooling you,

Some cop's Steph Curry with the shot...
'Cause no matter who's in front of you all you do is pull and shoot,
Then when it enters the net you use every excuse that's allowed,
It's online now and it happened at our home so that last shot just affected the crowd,
But cheering isn't what you hearing and it isn't a taste you could savor...
It's the HATE U GIVE that got us returning the favor!

By: Dilemma
A.k.a. StrokeGameVicious

SOMEBODY'S SON

Momma...
The last word I spoke while you choked the life out of me,
A black man that's sharp with a little "Jagged Edge" ain't threatening? "I
Gotta Be"
Honestly we tired of the apologies, equality is an anomaly,
We don't want help from the people killing us and cover it with lies,
No matter what I say our State meant for a statement to be meant for
whatever the State decides,
We waiting for change...but at what cost?
Because more than a quarter of us you shoot at the drop of a dime now
there's a penny for your thoughts,
The damages are damaging,
Getting away with killing blacks due to poor management,
While other cops stand still and watch...the disadvantage is,
We hoping they become an accessory to a body like a mannequin,
But win or lose...on both sides they getting bread...
They just meet in the middle like sandwiches,
See, they wear a badge to badger us...our lives they take away
So to make a change in a major way
We'll make them pay until we break the bank,
We the wrong color...no matter about freedom of speech or our march,
They don't see us through how we speak when we talk,
White is the light where laws believe there's no fault,
Then hate those who love us because they're nocturnal...
Because they don't understand what they see in the dark,
Before we get a cap and gown they'll cap us down,
Get away with it...then come back around to give our back a round,
I mean ask Jacob Blake...my fault you can't,
He barely want to speak 'cause you weak police feel free

To shoot first and rather cap a nigga (sigh) taking a knee,
You want non-violent protest? Let me paint a picture,
Yeah y'all "act" like y'all care...but you just making a scene,
You the biggest gang in the world until we get gangsta with ya,
l am Jacob Blake...now look what you done done,
Did you ever stop to think that l am someone's son?

By: Dilemma
A.k.a. StrokeGameVicious

YOUR ANTHEM

O say can you breathe...that's what Anthem said,

Not the National Anthem but my brother Anthem who understands how the anthem should be read,

Loyalty? To savages who ravage the less fortunate,

Then the media gets paid to expedite the footage to start endorsing it,

Then the news have the nerve to say "Our prayers are with you" and probably haven't prayed a day in your life,

Unless it had to do with those white stars and those broad stripes,

Death and destruction bodies laid out through the perilous fight,

It wasn't even the people who fought that we needed to show proof of life,

It was the bombs bursting in air and the flag still being there that gave proof through the night,

This is the anthem that is supposed to represent freedom from an enemy,

But what do you do when you find out the enemy is the inner me,

So when you look in the mirror you don't see who you are...I call that Vampiric tendencies,

My name may be Dilemma but you're the problem I'm not a kid anymore and I'm no longer timid,

So wherever this symbol lies it symbolizes the simple lies because freedom was just a figment,

You wanted me to give my allegiance to a cloth and because I ain't know any better I held my hand over my heart,

Recited the pledge thought we were indivisible not knowing that we were all so far apart,

If I'm lying someone just tell me I'm wrong,

Because of a racist comment in this poem we only sing 1/4 of the song,

The guy who wrote the song was a slave owner but we singing with glee,

Someone please tell Francis Scott Key not me I'll be taking a knee,

Due to my conscience I can't allow myself to believe in those words that I
use to say,
So yes...this is YOUR ANTHEM NOT MINE...THE LAND OF THE
KNEE AND HOME OF THE SLAVES!

By: Dilemma
A.ka. StrokeGameVicious

FREEDOM ISN'T

Aye Fredrick Douglas when you see Martin Luther King,
Tell him people still not woke and others are sleeping on his dream,
Because it's America no one's holding her accountable,
Fredrick Douglas said she's young and impressible...well it's money that's
getting her to suck the life right out of you,
Americas still getting paid to video slavery and it's still progressing,
Which basically shows that the press is still in the middle of oppression,
We see it enough and it's annoying because broadcasting it still isn't helping
a bit,
I've gotten a new sense of what a nuisance is since the news sent to give us a
noose to hang ourselves with,
We're still the same length away from each other as you were back then it's
exactly the same,
I mean yeah we came a long way...
But if we face to face moving forward and America's moving backwards the
distance still ain't changed,
Only location...freedom is up in the air and this flight's long,
Progression starts with progress but the end of it is what we have our eye on,
The Statue of Liberty was a nice gesture America but look at the way that
she's faced,
Back turned and New York City and Jersey City argued over the jurisdiction
it's placed,
Nothing new for two people arguing over a female this way...
But how ironic...because we still fighting for the same freedom today,
But is she worth it?
Hell yeah! Even if the cause cause an effect to happen for generations to
come,
I want my kids to know I ain't turn a blind eye until freedom has won,

Some people may take offense or think I'm being mean to you but what's racism really mean to you,

When you fighting over a block or color when freedom isn't free to do,

And you're still slaves to the whip and your actions still means you're bruised,

Except you're taking it out on each other instead of the people we needing to,

Because we need you to...

We can't do this without support from our own we have to continue to be different,

I don't know how it feels so I can't tell you what freedom is, but I can tell you what it isn't...

This!

By: Dilemma
A.k.a. StrokeGameVicious

CHRISTIAN DIVIDED BY RELIGION

There's lots of division amongst Christians,
And because we know everything we forgot how to listen,
That's not fair to start,
That's careless at heart,
How are we supposed to be closely knitted when you're the part of the body
tearin' us apart?
But you the choir to admire,
The Deacon of the weekend,
The Pastor of the Master,
You play that role real well...you deserve an Oscar for that acting,
Stop it...you a prophet looking for profit,
You use the Church for your perch,
The knowledge that we acknowledge,
Should be polished for the cursed,
Yet when the Father is emerged,
We want solace when it hurts...
But when what we want is not in His Will...We wanna wallow in the dirt,
Then use that same dirt...to throw on the next man,
Just to screw that person over just like a sex scam,
We want what's best for us not the person you sittin' next to,
Because you're next to nothing and if I'm nothing I wouldn't expect you to,
Ain't none of exempt from being cursed in a place of peace,
We all supposedly "live" off the blood of Jesus...
And as Christians we are to embrace the leech,
We act like a parasite when God wants to repair our sight,
To stare at Christ...the Glaring Light,
But we rather carry stripes instead of life,
That's backwards..
But see you all about the Sword in the House of The Lord,

But wanna act sooo shallow...that you could drown on the shore,
But sure you got it all figured out,
Take it to scripture because Proverbs 1 shows the public,
Be who you are...not who you hang around...
Because no telling who you trying to be when I ain't around,
Regardless of who's right or wrong let criticism be constructive,
Don't assume be humble and live above it,
That the fear of the Lord is knowledge and fools despise wisdom and instruction,
Is that you? What about you?
Yep...because we all think we know it all and I know someone right now hates hearing the truth,
So if anyone's offended my apolo...naw...'cause most likely I'm talking to you...
Now before you clap I don't want to take full credit as the author,
Because while you're thanking me I'm thanking my Father

By: Dilemma
A.k.a. StrokeGameVicious

NOTE 2 SELF

I know from the angle you're at you have a look of disgust,

But I know from experience things will straighten out once you adjust,

It's just mistakes are made,

Feelings are vague,

But because love is essential God'll make a way,

There's more to you than what meets the eye,

You give me a peace of mind,

That aids in that peace of mine,

Regardless of what anyone think of you,

Just know that they think of you,

And should be thanking you,

You're one of a kind,

Others thinking there has to be flaws,

There's lines of raw material mind engulfed with words of pure methodical thought,

You're Samson when his strength regained,

David when the Giant was slain,

Joseph locked up in chains,

Meshack Shadrack and Abindigo surviving flames,

A Child of God...

Misunderstood yet ready to accept the consequences for odd decisions,

The cost of living had you crossing bridges...not burning them,

But the mistakes you made had you learn from 'em,

So now you've grown for compassion and to show Love,

With no grudge so don't ever hold on to what God let go of,

That's not you...

I know it may seem as if you let your family down,

But it ain't about what you were it's about what you can be now,

Put on that same Armor of God...they hand me downs,

Even though it feels we enslaved,

Being brave is in your DNA,

You can't give up...it's not you,

Just because you have nobody to give you support back like a barstool,

With your words you've brought people on this journey with you like a carpool,

Everyone's not going to like you because there's only one like you...Dilemma!

By: Dilemma
A.k.a. StrokeGameVicious

LOVE UNSEALED

dedicated to Lamarea

I loved you before I even knew you existed,
I took the coward road by staying my distance,
I just want you to forgive me
For not holding you up when you needed me the most,
For not taking responsibility for my actions. To you I was a ghost,
You are my heart and soul,
Without you this pain unfolds,
And it hurts like hell
Without you I'm on this lonely road
Keep your head held high and if you ever feel you're alone,
Just know that I'll always love you more than anything
And I'll eventually be home.

By: Dilemma
A.k.a. Your Father

GOD ONLY KNOWS

Your past is present for future gain,

I believe,

What you think of me does not define me,

Time speaks for itself you're not the same as you used to be,

You used to be a use to,

Something you were used to until Jesus used others to prove that HE can use you too,

This is temporary...forget a road paved in gold,

A body of dust and old,

A mansion that rusts and mold,

And a heart that lusts and cold,

I mean 32 below...

Has kilt our pride and shifts our lives to one side,

What's going on in this head of ours? Empty...we done lost our mind,

But God only knows how to straighten us out not later but sooner,

Imminent danger a fool us look at Satan...He gave him an inch and he thought he was the ruler,

That's because of what we've built up inside,

How can you set your sight on things above with yo head down?

Jesus says lean on me and it's not a Joe Clark speech,

Let that cold heart speak truth the Lord sees the hurt and pain...

But it's worth the gain...

It may be cloudy but there's flowers in the mist,

His power is immense,

He empowers and uplifts,

He's been through the wilderness and never cowards in the tent,

My...God...reigns!..that's why He showers you with gifts,

But God only knows who you truly are...mean the real you,

Not the pretend around my friends to fit in you,

But the compassionate softest heart that Jesus could fit in you...you,
You...you...and you too and you two,
Remember the phrase I'm a kick you where the sun don't shine?
Well there's not a place on my body where the Son don't shine,
He has set the precedent and though my body is decadent
It is evident that He is now a resident,
The only Good in me is in skin deep,
He conquered the grave so what's 6 feet?
Height and length,
A measurement only measured by the measurer,
But God's LOVE can't be measured not even by a plethora,
It's extending that same LOVE when you think you have nothing left,
Until under your breath all I hear is...

By: Dilemma
A.k.a. StrokeGameVicious

DEFINITION OF LOVE

It could be a heart-pounding sensation from the sight of a life unknown,
Through visual stimulation of seeds yet unsown,

Electromagnetic pulses from the stroke of movement,
With an unusual feeling that's so elusive,

A reason to break the usual routine because of an individual,
An emotion that's steadily growing and indispensable,

A prayer for someone we hopin' that pulls through,
Or as easy as a laugh that fills a dull room,

An uplifting conversation that boggles the mind,
As simple as a walk on the beach...it could be a product of time,

It's as gentle as the comforting of a mother,
It could even be the suffering for another,

It extends to great depths...and deaths...and there's no back buttons,
It's provided many causes of suicide...all because the lack of it,

Just as there's pros there's cons, it doesn't discriminate,
Because what it means to one person can be interpreted as hate,

A moment where life itself stands still...your heart rapidly beating
repeatedly.
Or even the chastisement to better someone deprived of human decency,

That feeling when your significant other sees you with amazement,

From the eye contact where your souls meet with deep gazing.

An action brought upon by some type of attraction that you're willing to invest in,
A yearning desire for something that can only be fulfilled by this object of affection,

A light at the end of a tunnel to escape darkness,
It comes from a place where some ventricles are stationed...continuously touched by a marksman,

I've experienced it all...so who's to say this is Love? I wonder...
Because the true definition of love will always be defined by the lover.

By: Dilemma
AkA. StrokeGameVicious

MY FIRST BORN

dedicated to Indemiona Jones

Indemiona I love you more than you'll ever know. I can't apologize enough to you for not being there when you needed me most. I can only take responsibility for my mess ups.

2 much 2 bear,

2 little 2 understand,

2 young 2 see I was 2 stubborn 2 be a man,

2...

The age I left but never forgot about you,

Couldn't wait to see what you'd amount to,

Regardless of how much time I have I rather do life without parole than life without you,

Indemionia you're my first born...the better half of me,

What you have of me is capturing the path you seek to build a masterpiece,

You deserve more than what I could give...

I let my pride divide your mom and I and I regret every moment away from you,

Not knowing how you were doing yet your mom made a way for you,

But wait,

If you're upset because of how you got to wait now,

Don't let the pressure of me being in here be a weight now,

'Cause if you let this hold you in place...then you'll stay down,

Hold your head up...You're my Princess but also a Queen,

The lack of my physical being is a momentary thing,

I hate that as a father I'm not there for you because I grew up the same way,

Thinking my father a deadbeat dad...but here I am digging my own grave,

I have no excuses...

Knowing what I know now...it was predicted that a high percentage of black men would end up in prison,

That was trending way before trending got so much attention,

I just don't want you to look at me different,

Because my geographical position is only distance,

We still can become close...

Building a relationship with you is more important than any struggle I had growing up,

I know it's rough I thought I knew everything when I ain't know enough,

Just open up. Tell me about YOU...

Yeah I know at the time I committed...to hear about you and your interest...yet being behind all these fences was not my intention,

Yes Princess I remember...

When you cried in my arms,

Saying you wanted to get to know ME! that left a sharp pain in my heart,

You just wanted US time

And now I'm asking that you give us time

Because I know your time is precious but for you...I'm always willing to give up mine,

You are everything and more...

You're one of God's greatest gift to me...My first born!

By: Dilemma
A.k.a. Your Father

KING

Where do I begin when I don't feel like a man? Man!

I just don't want you to think I am a piece of shit!

But I do want to be honest with you because you deserve the truth,

Because your mom and I weren't in the right place...

I was never invited to the delivery room,

It's not her fault or yours it's mine and I take responsibility as the man of the house,

That I did not do what it took to take care of my spouse,

But don't let our mistakes dictate your future planning now!

YOU ARE A KING!

Of the Most High God...King of All!

A natural-born leader with qualities beyond measure,

Whether or not I am in or out of your life should not stop you from being better,

Better as in better than the negative around you that surround you,

Shine when darkness has seemed to overcrowd you,

And only add positivity and see what you amount to,

YOU ARE A KING!

The moment I held you was one of the greatest days of my life,

Another part of me was you!

Your sisters and brothers too,

Even for the brief moment I held you was enough to last a lifetime,

I was young and dumb and thought I was having fun but wasn't in my right mind,

I wanted to be a millionaire but never took advantage of the lifelines,
Don't be like me be better...treat a woman like a Queen because...

YOU ARE A KING!

By: Dilemma
A.k.a. Your Father

TEARS THROUGH A BROKEN MIRROR

dedicated to In'Dayvionia Washington and Michael Lyric Beam

I hate to see the tears that I've brought you...that wasn't my intention,
Now the tension is emotional and you've become the victim,
I let you down and I'm not there to comfort you when you need it,
I'm not around during your accomplishments and achievements,
I can't believe it...
It's time that I take time while doing time to reminisce,
From the time you were born and all the time that we spent,
And in time all of this will pass and things will be different,
To where I'm not being dogged...just because I'm behind a few fences,
Now Listen...
You've always been the reason I push to be the best at what I do,
Because what I do best is push and the reason has always been YOU!
I mean there's no other way to explain it,
I'm so anxious to see you succeed in everything you claiming,
You're on a different level...you see it's just like an apartment,
And losing you made me realize what being apart meant,
I couldn't see you,
Son I won't say no names but they know who they are,
God watches out for His children...especially those you scar,
I'm nervous...
Because of how much you've both grown and how much I've missed,
You're God's Gift and without Him you wouldn't exist...
So Lord I thank you...for this Masterpiece you knitted together while in
their mother's womb,
So perfectly put together with my looks...yet in the same Image as YOU,
You both truly are an inspiration and I admire your ambition to be fully
educated,

Soft-hearted and forever gracious that no matter where I am our
relationship is worth saving,
And I Thank You,
Because I know firsthand how hard it is to be without your father,
But I was on my way to hell and God gave me another option,
It may not be what I wanted but it is exactly what I needed,
Because the ways of this world were truly my only teachings,
I can see it...and just know I want nothing but the best for you,
Even though right now it may seem like me being gone is not the best
for you,
I care for you...that's why speaking about how much I love you is so
effortless,
The poetry just flows and your heart is where my treasure is,
I'm better than I was but I don't ever plan on settlin',
But keep your head up and know that you both are Heaven Sent,
This is only for the moment no matter how long that moment is,
Because the most precious moments are the moments that we give,
I LOVE YOU In'Dayvionia and Lyric

By: Dilemma
A.k.a. Your Father

IMAGES

Lies, deceit, fake, so it's the trust you ruined,

So I trust you to do exactly what I don't trust you doing,

You supposed to be different...please, you far from that,

Thought you were adding spice to my life but was pouring salt so you can start from scratch,

I spend nights alone...and when you're home you're on the phone talking to God know who,

But I know you...it had to be some ole dude ooooo...girl don't get me started,

You fuckin' him huh? Be honest?

Is he better than me? I knew it...I'm always trying to please you and this the thanks I get,

Thanks...I get it...you just want something different,

You see something you like and wonder how it'd feel to hit it,

You no good give it up to the whole hood hood rat,

And your excuse is: this is actually something I'm good at,

Why? After I've sacrificed so much..

I've ignored females who make passes at me when they passing me...I could get even,

But I flash the ring to make it known I'm taken like Liam Neeson,

And scary me asked you to marry me what was I thinking?

I'm in love...and it's the love in me that could end me,

Because I got so much to give to not reciprocate with envy,

I told you I was insecure and felt I wasn't good enough,

Now I finally understand why we haven't made love in months,

People told me about you and I can always tell who is and ain't my friends,

Cuz they read me like a license plate...so they can always tell what state I'm in,

Now I finally understand why I can see things clearer,
It's self-reflection so now I guess I'll get my ass out this mirror...

By: Dilemma
A.k.a. StrokeGameVicious

I'M LISTENING

I make mistakes Lord but why me?

Haven't I been through enough stuff?

Don't I write good music so people could bump to it?

Do I not give you the repetition of recognition you deserve?

Am I not keeping my eyes on the sparrow because the straight and narrow seems curved?

You couldn't have helped my mom through addiction,

You're God! I'd expect that to be a given,

I grew up despised by some of the people that raised me...so what's the difference?

They didn't treat me no better...I was put out in the cold now where is the logic?

Homeless asking a random stranger through bars to use the phone...how ironic,

Where were you when I had nothing...it was cold facing those crooked with smiles,

I actually had skills to bust a rhyme but...look at me now,

My baby having a baby and I'm not there for support,

That makes me feel weak...but I'm supposed to carry my Sword!?

How!? I'm dying inside without my kids...l can't be the voice of reason,

Because those poisoned demons had me avoiding Jesus,

Your children come here for you not me...show yourself!

You don't need my help...

Look at me! I'm not fit to be a vessel for your praise,

They come to worship YOU...but they yelling my name,

How does that work Lord?

I don't want the responsibility the burden is way too much,

All this weight is on my shoulders...just from lifting you up,

Lord YOU'RE the finishing touch

Meaning they see YOU and me instead of YOU in me because YOU end me,
The Beginning and The End...The First and The Last,
Alpha and Omega...Future, Present, and the Past,
But where were you? Huh!?
My GOD I'm here for you but I just want to hear from you...

By: Dilemma
A.k.a. StrokeGameVicious

BETTER LATE THAN NEVER

You read me like a book...but who knew it'd be our final chapter?

Picturing you out of my life is something I don't capture,

But I put so much weight on your shoulders that it gave you a spinal fracture,

When I know I should've had your back like a chiropractor,

The best included waking up next to you,

But never knew what I had until I lost it and...that's when I lost it,

Now I'm going crazy...but I'm the one who caused it,

All because I wanted to...run away from Love...And now I'm exhausted,

Tossin' and turnin'...

All because our nights didn't exist

The life you entrenched,

That included us with kids and a white picket fence,

Is now a flight that's at risk,

Meaning it's going down...

And we bound to crash if we don't take control,

Because the things that overtakes our soul can break our mold,

And shatter everything that make us whole,

Our Faith was gold,

I know I'm just now figuring out how much you meant and it's like shattering dreams,

I killed that hazardous fiend to raise up that passionate me to recreate that Lazarus theme,

I hope it's not too late I know I done messed up but I can be enough,

No more running away from love...

Less rough...more loving...invest in us...

I'm sprinting now...what I kind of meant was I was a dick that's what a condom meant for us

A condiment meant...I'm just trying to catch up,
I've been late my entire life...
And I don't want to be left behind so this time I'm a make it right

By: Dilemma
A.k.a. StrokeGameVicious

A BEAUTIFUL MESS

A mind comprised of decisive literary thoughts brought to life through
speech,
Expressed through verbal communication to those who learn and teach,

A visual spokesman who brings to life the words engrained,
Derogatory or uplifting the gift still remains,

A cemetery of coffins often visited to reminisce the lost,
Empty with no engraved tombstones because I couldn't bury the thoughts,

An uninhabited Island naked and alone,
Judgement free unless I'm judging me but I can make it on my own,

A rollercoaster with no seatbelt which makes it invigorating,
From the twist and turns that provide life and death situations,

Some may think I've lost my mind and may need some help,
But I don't mind...it's the only place I don't have to clean up after myself,

Happiness, Arrogance, Sadness, Motivation, Determination, Amazed,
Enthusiasm, Excited, Contentious, Free, Enslaved,

All of which is included with others not mentioned like Pain,
I look at my work like *Wow...*
What a beautiful mess I've made

By: Dilemma
A.k.a. StrokeGameVicious